HOW TO WRITE A WINNING UCAS PERSONAL STATEMENT FOR STEM SUBJECTS

Bianca Khor

ISBN: 9798656968287

Cover design by Bianca Khor and Tan Ying Xin
Library of Congress Control Number: 2018675309
Printed in the United States of America

CONTENTS

AUTHOR'S NOTE

Dear Reader,

I wrote this book in the middle of the mandatory self-isolation period during the COVID-19 (coronavirus) pandemic in 2020, where I was lucky enough to have witnessed a few major events.

Firstly, it was amazing to learn how scientists of various disciplines have joined forces to combat the outbreak, whether it was through the numerous vaccine development efforts that required a strong foundation in biochemistry and physics, or design engineering to fashion a novel ventilator assisting infected patients with breathing difficulties. A sound understanding in mathematical biology, on the other hand, has assisted governments in the epidemiological modelling of the pandemic, providing valuable data to make informed decisions for their country's future action plans.

In other words, I believe it's fair to say that the power of science to resolve global issues has and will continue to fascinate me. Considering that you picked up this book, I would presume you have a desire or ambition to further your knowledge within the area of science (or STEM subjects as one may call it). And I would like to congratulate you for that.

STEM subjects are, arguably, not for the faint-hearted. With the level of brain-numbing *basics* and intricate details one is expected to know by heart before being able to (finally) build some "cool stuff", surely it wouldn't be too surprising for admission tutors (who probably got their fair share of mental constipation from these concepts 40 years ago, maybe even up until today) to expect a certain degree of awareness and calibre from you too.

With that in mind, the personal statement is a unique opportunity for you to demonstrate your commitment and passion towards the STEM subject of your choice, and this is where I hope my book could help you out with. This book has been structured in such a way where it offers a detailed step-by-step guide on what an ideal personal statement comprises. A critical analysis of personal statement samples written by various successful applicants have also been included, and I hope you're a big fan of comics (basically some light-hearted content) too.

Feeling motivated to craft an academic masterpiece? Let's get started.

Yours sincerely,
Bianca

ABOUT THIS BOOK

This book is designed to provide you with a comprehensive step-by-step guide on how you can stand out as an applicant through writing an excellent personal statement. Chapters 1 to 5 are loaded with snippets of actual personal statements written by successful students as part of their application to leading UK universities.

Chapter 1 gives a brief introduction to the basic details about a personal statement and allows you to gauge the importance of this piece of writing.

Chapter 2 helps you get a better idea of how you could write a compelling opening paragraph that grabs your readers' attention.

Chapter 3 offers suggestions to help you brainstorm ways in which you could tailor your personal statement to demonstrate an academic curiosity for your subject.

Chapter 4 supports you in ending your personal statement with a bang!

Chapter 5 constitutes full-length examples of actual personal statements written by successful applicants, summarising the learning points shared in the previous chapters.

Chapter 6 is filled with valuable tips and advice before you officially embark on your personal statement writing journey.

CHAPTER 1: THE PERSONAL STATEMENT

What is it?
To put it simply, the personal statement is an essay for you to sell yourself and to showcase your huge learning appetite. The catch is, you are given a maximum of 4,000 characters (approximately 500 words) and 47 lines to accomplish this.

As highlighted by top Russell Group universities, this presents an opportunity for applicants, in their own writing, to communicate their interests alongside any relevant experiences, achievements, and skillsets they've developed to demonstrate an unceasing academic curiosity for a specific subject area.

Why should you care?
Let's assume that you're aiming to win a place as a STEM student at an extremely "competitive" UK university, such as the University of Cambridge and Imperial College London.

Taking the Natural Sciences course offered by the University of Cambridge as our first example, the Admissions Office managed a total of 2,708 applications in 2019 and granted offers to 716 applicants. Whereas in 2018, 2,594 students across the world tried out for the same course, with 680 of them eventually becoming recipients of an offer letter. This gives us an application-to-offer ratio of four[1].

On the other hand, an aspiring Chemical Engineer would have found himself/herself competing against four other candidates for a place at Imperial College London in 2019, based on the 5:1 applications-to-admissions ratio indicated by the university[2].

Therefore, while it would be true for one to say that the personal statement forms only one section of a UCAS application, and that an excellent piece offers no panacea for a student's poor AS Level examination performance or a bad teacher's reference, it is crucial to understand that this essay could still provide a solid baseline for a competitive application. This would be extremely applicable especially in a scenario where admission tutors must select between two equally competent and deserving candidates (e.g. both having top predicted grades) due to the limitations of places the university is able to provide.

Meanwhile, universities like Oxbridge, along with courses such as Medicine and Dentistry, contain an interview component as part of their selection process. So, there is a high likelihood that the contents of your personal statement will be discussed. Suppose that you used your personal statement as a platform to highlight certain areas of interest within a subject, this would offer a plethora of opportunities for you to stand out as an enthusiastic candidate (and to your interviewer's delight!).

Henceforth, a good mindset when approaching the writing of your personal statement would be to see it as a *bonus tool* – it is supposed to aid you in the game of university applications, not hurt you.

What constitutes a good personal statement?

Simplicity. You do not need to be a walking Thesaurus who churns out dramatic-sounding vocabularies or sentences.

The recipe to a good personal statement comprises of three simple ingredients:

1. A well-thought-out structure that allows information to flow in a logical manner

2. A writing style which connects well with the readers' thought process

3. The inclusion of materials that align with the selection criteria of your selected universities

All in all, every single sentence should *add value* to your application as a strong candidate (to be discussed further in Chapter 3). The end goal of this writing is for you to effectively convince the admission tutor(s) that you know your stuff, and you've got what it takes to rock as a student at their educational institution.

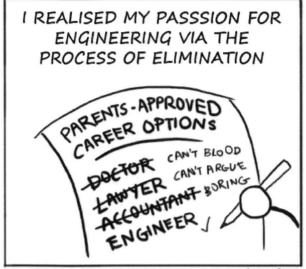

CHAPTER 2: MAKING AN ENTRANCE

What was the spark?
Imagine yourself in a situation where a good friend or a stranger walk up to you, and immediately questions: "why would you like to study Biomedical Engineering?". What is the first thing that pops up in your mind? And what would you tell them?

Maybe you were an avid scuba diver and was fascinated at how the echolocation in whales and dolphins has resulted in various nature-inspired innovations, such as the sonar systems in a fish-finder or medical equipment. If you are hydrophobic by nature and find yourself to be a biblio-phile instead, a good read from a profound inventor may have ignited your interests to develop a creative and prob-lem-solving mindset. Or it could be that spending your afternoons on a lecture series on YouTube or Coursera has left you craving to learn more about utilizing surface en-gineering and microbiology to tackle the global problem of antimicrobial resistance.

See what I did there?

All you really need to do, is to ask yourself "what is your defining moment" (or "what was the spark?", "what kinds of topics relating to your subject area made you forget to eat?") that inspired you to study a subject at an under-graduate level.

And oftentimes, one of the easiest ways to do so would be to reflect on your past experiences. Take note that it doesn't necessarily have to be an extracurricular activity which drives your decision-making process.

A person's cultural, socio-economic background, or hobbies could be an alternative source of ideas. A personal anecdote, in other words. An artificial intelligence and coding enthusiast may have witnessed his parents struggling to afford an expensive MRI scan in his childhood, and this fuelled him with the motivation to innovate new machines that permits a more cost-effective diagnosis.

Following that train of thought, another aspect for you to consider would be "what kinds of problems would you like to solve?". For example, one's superconductor obsession could have a desire to resolve heavy traffic congestions in a city with an underdeveloped public transport system, resulting in an application to read Physics. Even a mere activity such as building structures using Lego bricks may prompt someone to think about infrastructures and sustainability, leading them to consider a degree in Civil Engineering. Heck, online shopping on Amazon may be a great way to start thinking critically about consumer purchasing patterns and how we could best model it to help a company increase their profits, and a course in Data Science or Mathematics (with a focus on statistics) would be an excellent rabbit hole into the world of numbers and patterns.

If you find yourself to be struggling to come up with a few solid reasons for studying your chosen subject – as brutal as it may sound, this would be a clear indication of your lack of passion for your course, and it may be a good idea for you to reconsider your options.

Spare the waffle (we don't have the maple syrup to go with it)
You might have heard some of these statements:

"Please do not start with a cliché sentence like 'ever since the age of five'..."

"Do not exaggerate or invent stories..."

"Avoid the use of bombastic or overly-fancy words..."

"Do not include irrelevant quotations made by famous people..."

Those are fair statements. You can equate admissions tutors to sceptics if that helps you prioritise your materials better. It is highly possible that they are overworked individuals, with a tendency to be extremely critical towards any overstated claims regarding a long-lasting dream of becoming a medicinal chemist as well as relatively unrealistic documentations such as encountering and completing the original "Principia Mathematica" series by Isaac Newton at the age of fourteen.

An "influential person" in your life, which could be anyone ranging from Bill Gates to your Chemistry teacher to your local physician, is another interesting angle for you to look at. However, do bear in mind that it is important for you to draw strong links between these people and their quotes or actions *directly and explicitly* with your subject area, and how that got you interested. This would be a much more effective approach compared to quoting something random they said in the news just for the sake of sounding smart. This would also be applicable to any interesting questions which you may consider writing about – talk about what gave rise to your thinking, what you did to find the answer(s), and what did you conclude.

It might also be worthwhile to note that there are certain quotes that "famous people" *didn't* say. A great example: "I fear the day that technology will surpass our human interaction. The world will have a generation of idiots." Nope that wasn't Albert Einstein, that was the Internet.

Make sure you do your research well.

Essentially...
Remember, this is not an investor pitch nor a talent audition that demands a high level of charisma or drama to excite the judges within seconds. Admission tutors look out for a *background* story that demonstrates enough curiosity to study your subject at a tertiary education level, whilst generating insightful thoughts towards the various issues or big topics surrounding it.

Some students have also pointed out that working on the introduction last as it may help their writing flow better with the body of their personal statement, given that a better vision would have been established by then. But of course, this is dependent on your writing style and preferences, so just do what works best for you.

Otherwise trust me, it is as straightforward as it sounds. The main element that makes up a good introduction would be individuality. It is about who you are as a person, why do you care about your subject, and questions or opinions you may have about it (which you hope your university course could provide educational support with).

No one else will have exactly the same experiences and

thought process as you, and that is the biggest asset you have!

Time for a deep dive
To help you to get a better idea on what we've just discussed, here are a few opening paragraphs of successful personal statements.

> **Biochemistry** - *When I lost my grandmother to lymphoma, it struck me that my parents were paying so much for her care. While we were fortunate enough to be able to afford it, I was sure many others were unable to, and that shouldn't be the case. While the scientists who bring us these drugs deserve remuneration and the cost of manufacturing it may be high, it shouldn't come at the cost of its affordability and depriving millions of access to it. I believe Biochemistry is the answer to tearing down this barrier to medical care and giving everyone the chance at life they deserve.*

What makes this paragraph interesting?
Essentially, the applicant managed to demonstrate an awareness as well as understanding of a critical global problem, and effectively linked the issue to his/her subject. Interestingly, the applicant proposed that his/her area of study would hold the key to resolving the identified problem. This effectively showcased some independent thinking or originality, which may serve as a gripping point to "hook" the reader (i.e. the admissions tutor) into wanting to learn more about the applicant's reasonings behind their statement. It also brings up a fascinating topic for discussion during the interview stage (if there is one).

Biomedical Engineering - The ground-breaking biomedical technology of rotationplasty helped Gabi Shull, an osteosarcoma survivor who had her right leg amputated to achieve the most unimaginable things like dancing. Those endless possibilities created by engineers and the unthinkable achievements the human species can make to overcome obstacles through knowledge, experiments and discoveries. Dancing is inseparable from my childhood. I deeply relate to her passion and eagerness to pursue art in dancing. Biomedical technologies had already given her brilliant opportunities to enjoy doing what she loves and to inspire countless numbers of people. Although Gabi's case is just an example of the many people who face medical and physical difficulties, I sincerely wish to have the chance to contribute my efforts to help more of them to pursue their dreams.

What makes this paragraph interesting?

You may not realise this about yourself, but everyone will have their own unique stories to tell (no matter how much you may deny it). In fact, your story really does not need to be something super amazing, it just has to be about you – whether the event is big or small.

In this snippet, the applicant did a great job at exhibiting his/her enthusiasm and passion for their subject, whilst linking it to a long-established hobby. Besides that, the passing reference on the rotationplasty technology would indirectly suggest the applicant has been keeping themselves well-informed of the latest biomedical technological advances. This may also imply their consistent engagement with his/her subject.

Civil Engineering - A roller coaster ride excites an adventurous kid like me. In the amusement park, apart from thrill and excitement felt from the rides, what caught my eyes is the structure of the track. Rhetorical questions came across my mind while observing the construction. I was amazed by the way pillars of steel were planted on to the ground and further joined together to form tracks that can withstand high speed cars that are safe to hop on. Extended readings and research on this unfolded my interest towards the construction of buildings, bridges, roads and railways. Even as simple as the shelter that protected us from devastation of nature involved the sweat of civil engineers. I realise how important a building serves as a main infrastructure before electricity and machines are fitted in.

What makes this paragraph interesting?
In this case, the applicant showcased an awareness of the ubiquitous applications of their subject in our daily lives, ultimately demonstrating an appreciation for civil engineering. Hence, if you are finding yourself struggling to think of a good problem or hobby to write about, this is another noteworthy angle to consider.

Geology - From mountains to seas, from cities to the countryside, from Earth's crust to its core, they possess different geological characteristics. Plenty of Earth's natural phenomena can be explained by our experience and understanding in Geology. Thus, this subject has provided invaluable assistance to major industries such as mining, construction and agriculture. For example, one must determine the geological factors of the land and soil before constructing a skyscraper or a mere house to ensure maximum safety. It is widely known that the state of our environment can take its toll on our health. Through our expertise, plenty of environmental-friendly protocols can be introduced to the general public. With the Chartership of the Geology Society that I hope to obtain, I wish to be part of this field to induce more radical improvements in terms of technological development and to raise awareness among mankind to be the big change in environment conservation.

What makes this paragraph interesting?

The applicant did a terrific job at emphasizing how having a sound knowledge foundation in geology is essential before any real estate projects can be initiated. This statement exhibits their observation skills whilst providing a smooth transition to the next section, where the applicant explains their desire in obtaining the necessary qualifications to further their career in a geology-related field.

Key takeaway messages

When you are writing your introduction:

(1) Think about what is the defining moment that ignited your interest for your chosen subject

(2) Make sure all of your statements directly relate to your subject

(3) Bear in mind that an excellent introduction is all about explaining why do YOU care about your subject

IF PERSONAL STATEMENTS WERE HONEST #2

CHAPTER 3: DEMONSTRATING INTELLECTUAL CURIOSITY

What the heck is "intellectual curiosity"? Another typical buzzword in the university applications world, I know. But it's an important one, so let's dissect this term a little bit more:

An *intellectually curious* student would be one who has a persistent desire to learn how something functions, unafraid to venture into largely unexplored areas of a broad subject, or even to challenge normal practices with the intention of introducing innovative possibilities through unconventional thinking[3].

Let's view this from the perspective of scientists.

In the world of research, much of the industry progress is driven by having a question: "could we develop a faster method to detect tuberculosis in patients?", "how could we grow maize better to increase global food security?", "could we re-engineer cyanobacteria to produce plastic in replacement of the regular fossil fuel-based approach?" This ultimately results in the development of new experimental initiatives, research proposals, or even business ideas that could help resolve long-existing problems that have plagued humanity for decades. As you may have guessed it – with curiosity, we get good questions.

Academics and employers therefore are always in search

of bright and independent thinkers who are eager to boost their scientific literacy through continuous exploration and learning. As Harvard Business Review has described, corporates also value this trait as it effectively challenges an individual's critical thinking ability and cultivates an innovative spirit, thus allowing them to adapt within a dynamic industry as well as maintain a competitive advantage.[4]

Going beyond the taught material
Within the middle section of a UCAS personal statement, Russell Group universities typically prefer a 75 to 90%: 10 to 25% split between academic achievements (which you may have come across as "super-curricular" or "supra-curricular activities") and extracurricular activities. Most students tend to go for an 80:20 split, but that is really up to your own judgement.

This is the chance for you to exhibit a high degree of intellectual curiosity for your subject.

In addition to that, this is another area where admission tutors could get a better understanding on how you are as a student – are you the type who requires a lot of guidance, or are you an independent learner who takes the initiative to make things happen (or get things done)?

Always remember that academic potential is the top criteria set by the admissions tutors. Many candidates make the mistake of viewing this as a space to write a laundry list of personal achievements.

Therefore, the crucial part of this section would be making sure that every single line of your personal statement *adds value* to your reader (i.e. the admissions tutor). A good general practice for you would be to, at the end of each line, ask yourself "so what?" – does the sentence tell them why you love your subject and/or present a legitimate evidence to validate your claims?

To begin with, academic activities (in this case) are experiences you have had which enabled a substantial engagement with your subject area beyond the A Level/International Baccalaureate/other qualifications' syllabus, based on a thought-provoking topic that you came across during your studies.

For example, a prospective Biological Sciences applicant may have come across a brief text on the wonders of immune system in their biology textbook, and from there do outside reading on the complicated yet highly organised biological system, learn about the current research efforts on reengineering white blood cells to combat ovarian cancer through online courses on platforms like Udemy, edX and FutureLearn, or perhaps listen to educational podcasts discussing medical ethics and its implications towards healthcare-related businesses.

Furthermore, keeping yourself updated with the latest news on your subject along with other ongoing industrial, cultural, or public affairs is also another critical habit to practise. You could even consider writing a research article or completing an Extended Project Qualification (EPQ) to further convey an excitement in science and a willingness to learn. Visiting science museums may be an entertaining trip too, perhaps?

The main aim of these suggestions is to give you an idea on how you could go beyond the classroom syllabus to further your understanding of your subject.

Another thing that you should always bear in mind - every statement you make ought to have an appropriate evidence/learning point to back that up (thus *adding value* to your work). For example, there is simply no point for you to write about having a passion for game theory and probability, if you cannot elaborate on your insights or opinions regarding the topic despite having attended actuarial events at prestigious universities like the London School of Economics.

Again, let's take a look at a few personal statement snippets as a point of reference.

> ***Biological Sciences*** *- Recently, I spent a month in Madagascar helping scientists research and conserve biodiversity in wet and dry forests. Undergoing forest plots and distance sampling helped me develop statistical skills required for conservation. However, it was the endemic animals' charm that led me to research how they had adapted to their exclusive habitat. What struck me was the incredible dead-leaf mimicry of the Satanic Leaf-tailed gecko– camouflage artistically refined over millennia of natural selection. Chameleons, by contracting or expanding their skin, disturb the structural arrangement of nanocrystals in different specialised pigmented chromatophore cells, causing vivid colour changes with mood, temperature and territorial invasion. This initial interest in animal physiology led me to discover Eric Widmaier's "Why Geese Don't Get Obese", making me appreciate how creatively organisms have evolved in response to environmental stimuli. For example, additional air sacs along lung linings in*

Bar-headed geese allow easy soaring over the oxygen deprived peaks of the Himalayas. These adaptations prompted me to read Frances Ashcroft's "Life at The Extremes" to understand how humans have adapted to harsh environments.

What makes this paragraph interesting?

It is definitely a plus point for applicants to gain some work or research experience that directly relates to their subject. Nevertheless, this experience only really counts if the applicant can highlight the subject-relevant skills or knowledge they have gained (which was statistical analysis skills in this scenario)

Another interesting point to note is that the applicant had a very coherent style of writing, whereby he/she has communicated how the research experience has prompted their wider reading in certain topics via a logical manner.

This is extremely important in the scientific community as it helps the readers to develop an appreciation for your work and its global significance. Therefore, as a rule of thumb - scientists reward conciseness and coherence.

Chemistry - To gain a deeper understanding of the chemical composition of food, I dedicated my Extended Essay on exploring the concentration of vitamin C (also known as ascorbic acid) in orange juice. Over the course of nearly three months, I tried different methods to measure the ascorbic acid levels in orange juice. I began with using acid-base titration to produce a titration curve followed by ultraviolet–visible spectroscopy, both of which were unsuccess-

ful. It was finally when I used iodine redox titration whereby the ascorbic acid content was successfully determined. Although the research process was lengthier and more arduous than expected, I remain grateful for this experience as I never gave up. I learnt to perceive the failures encountered as part of the process. Not only did this experience teach me critical problem-solving skills, but it has also cultivated my inquisitive nature to seek knowledge beyond the scope of textbooks. Ultimately, this project has shaped me into a mature, persevering, responsible, and meticulous scientist.

What makes this paragraph interesting?
The applicant describes their experiences in research that has given them a taste of life as a food chemist. The description of his/her journey to determining the most suitable laboratory technique for measuring the ascorbic acid concentration was not over-exaggerated, and the applicant pointed out how he/her perseverance has allowed them to reach his end goal. This ultimately exhibits a great level of engagement and curiosity.

One possible way to strengthen this statement, if the character limit allows, would be for the applicant to write about potential reasons explaining why the acid-base titration and ultraviolet–visible spectroscopy did not work, or elaborate on how the use of iodine redox titration has mitigated the issues associated with the other two techniques.

Mechanical Engineering - *During my AS course, I have become interested in pursuing a mechanical en-*

gineering course due to my enthusiasm for Physics and Mechanics which are so intertwined. Although they are said to be challenging, I always find them so interesting particularly in topics like conservation of energy, calculation of forces in equilibrium, motion in circles and laws of gravity. Using the Mathematics knowledge that I have gained, I have learnt to solve problems in Physics by thinking out of the box and being creative in finding solutions using laws and principles I have learnt. The thirst to learn applications of theories have made mechanical engineering an ideal course not only for my future degree but also for my lifetime career. The A level course also provides opportunities to do practical work and hands-on projects which allow me to polish my skills in researching and analysing data independently in the labs. Coming up with my own solutions and ideas can be so tough and challenging but I manage to solve it with proper analysis to reach my goals. Making use of the skills provided, they will be useful and vital during my journey into becoming a mechanical engineer.

What makes this paragraph interesting?
This paragraph effectively conveyed the applicant's excitement and curiosity for their subject through making references to their STEM-oriented A Level subject combination whilst discussing the specific topics that they have found to be captivating for each subject. Other than that, the applicant demonstrated evidence of their understanding of the interdependence between these subjects by showing how the knowledge gained for one subject (in this case, mathematics) can be directly applied to crack a

problem tied to a different subject (which was physics).

Natural Sciences - Those who spend time outside in Borneo understand the irritation of mosquitoes. Interestingly we do not feel the bites as mosquitoes have one pair of serrated needles which minimise contact with nerves, something I learnt at a talk by Dr. Moshrefi-Torbati on biomimicry. Auxiliary reading showed that the adaptation was the basis on which engineer Seiji Aoyagi created his pain free hypodermic needle. The talk made me wonder about the other instances of biomimicry in nature. Inspired, I undertook an EPQ researching the topic. An example would be the tasar silkworm, whose silk fibroin is the main component of certain heart scaffolds as the silk is biocompatible while being able to degrade safely. The EPQ has refined my ability to conduct independent research which I applied to expand my understanding on respiration. For instance, I made notes on the ten steps of glycolysis as I had not been satisfied with the simplified version learnt in class.

What makes this paragraph interesting?

Here the applicant exhibited his/her initiatives to engage with their subject through attending academic seminars and then doing wider reading as part of their EPQ coursework. In particular, the applicant did a splendid job at linking what he/she learnt from the lecture to the EPQ as part of exploring a particular topic in biomimicry. This effectively explained their motivations behind choosing their EPQ topic, making the flow of the story smooth while simultaneously building up momentum for the applicant to write about what they learnt from all these experiences.

If the character limit permits, a suggested area of improvement for this snippet would be to elaborate on any new perspectives or scientific concepts that the applicant might have developed/came across during their journey, and whether this led to, or how this justifies, any alterations in their work narrative.

From ordinary to extraordinary (it all starts with you)
It would be reasonable to hear that top universities already expect applicants to take part in some of the aforementioned super-curricular activities. Theoretically, anyone could do all of those.

And this would mean that you are not unique enough.

This leads us to discuss other possible activities that you could do to help yourself stand out further from the massive pool of applicants.

Work experience is a popular option. You could try cold emailing as many organisations as possible to arrange a work shadowing placement or an internship. You could also leverage your school network to connect with a potential employer. However, do remember that your work experience must be related to your subject. This means that you shouldn't just find a random internship for the sake of mentioning that you have had some work experience!

To provide some context, let's imagine that you're a prospective Chemistry applicant. Following that train of thought, admission tutors would therefore place greater value on detailed accounts regarding an interesting Khan

Academy lecture discussing the many application of Le Chatelier's principle, for example, over a part-time job as a clerk.

Alternatively, if you would like to learn more about a research-focused career through a laboratory internship, you can easily obtain the email addresses of different Principal Investigators in the departmental page of a university website, whereby each university would have their own exclusive combinations of research themes.

Active participation in competitions, such as state-level science fairs or international tournaments like the International Mathematical Olympiad and the World Schools Debating Championships, are also perfect ways to gain greater exposure. Alternatively, attending a Summer School programme alongside spending your evenings at several academic conferences may be a good indicator that you are a keen and independent learner, who is capable of coping with an academically intensive learning environment.

However, please remember it is not about the number of experiences or events you had. Neither would the admissions tutor be impressed with all the student titles/positions you may have... if you are unable to draw relevant insights from your experiences.

A good personal statement effectively shares two important aspects with the reader:

(1) **What have you done to engage with your subject?**

In particular, what motivated you to do it? How does that experience connect to your current or future studies?

(2) **What new ideas or opinions you have developed regarding your subject area through your participation in these events?**

Ask yourself: did it change you as a person, surprise, or make you aware of something you never thought of before? What else would you want to know more about? With this knowledge, what actions did you/could you take to further develop your ideas?

Admissions tutors would love to welcome students who ask many questions whilst taking the initiative to search for new answers. A relatively detailed account of your learnings implies a passionate and intellectually curious individual. It also demonstrates that you're well-informed about your subject due to sound research and analytical abilities.

Moreover, they also like to see a person with an open mind and have the capability to develop logical arguments for or against a certain topic.

To help you get a better understanding of what I meant, let's take another deep dive into a few successful examples.

> *Biomedical Science - Beyond classes, I completed a work shadowing scheme in a biomedical company SurExam Biotech, which gave me an insight into the practical use of Biomedical Sciences as well as introduced me to haematology. I learned how biomedical scientists sequence the cancer patient's genome to monitor the dynamic of tumours and help oncologists to make recommendations for prescrib-*

ing medication. For instance, the circulating tumour cells (CTCs) scanning that they were doing on osteosarcoma using a machine called CanPatrol, which scans the CTCs and translates the results to the computer for scientists to characterise them according to their staining. Based on the CTC counts and the ratio of different types, scientists could then find the correlation with the Enneking stage and the tumours' distant metastases.

What makes this paragraph interesting?
The relatively comprehensive account of the work shadowing experience carries the impression that the applicant was fully engaged with their role. It also implies his/her high level of intellectual curiosity to better understand how CTC scanning can help clinicians to provide solid data-backed treatment recommendations for cancer patients.

If you are currently doing an internship or work placement related to your subject, the main takeaway message is for you to not only think about what you have learnt from this invaluable experience, but ideally to also consider how your learnings align with existing theories or laboratory techniques that you may come across at university. Alternatively, your learnings could serve as an idea springboard for wider reading materials.

Biotechnology *- Shadowing at a community pharmacy has surprised me, as the ultimate aim of pharmacists is to reduce patients' reliance on medicines. We should stimulate and enhance the body's own healing power instead of passively suppressing the* *harm done. By differentiation of blastemal cells, an entire starfish can be regenerated from one arm. Humans had that ability in the womb using pluripotent embryonic stem cells. They later become tissue-specific so repair is limited to certain body parts to prevent mass differentiation that might result in overgrowth. If we could reactivate our regenerative capabilities without unleashing the cancer process, losses and injuries can be fixed, utilising the potential of our complex genome.*

What makes this paragraph interesting?
Through the observation of a key issue during his/her work shadowing experience, the applicant managed to exhibit independent thinking by elaborating about a potential area of research he/she has in mind to resolve the problem.

A possible improvement point would be for the applicant to describe what else he/she needs to know more about in order to address the problem, or perhaps the plausible action plans that could be undertaken to build upon their idea.

Chemistry - Aside from theoretical knowledge, I also gained memorable practical experience. Last summer, I interned in a medicinal chemistry laboratory in Sichuan University for two weeks. I was part of the research and development team for a neotype contraceptive pill, which utilized high-performance liquid chromatography (HPLC) and gas chromatography (GC) to detect the purity of raw materials. What impressed me the most was my discussion with a professor regarding the reasons for obtaining inaccurate results of the samples' purities. After putting forward our own speculations and obtaining further data by conducting multiple groups of controlled trials, we eventually found that weighing inaccuracy caused data errors. Therefore, a new weighing method was designed to minimise the error. This unaccustomed process made me understand that scientific research is painstaking yet fulfilling.

What makes this paragraph interesting?
Another important rule of thumb to bear in mind is that – less is more. This means that you're better off writing a detailed description of one academically relevant experience compared to jotting down a long list of many irrelevant ones.

In this snippet, the applicant showcased analytical and problem-solving skills by elaborating on how he/she identified a problem and then proposed suitable experiments to troubleshoot the issue. There is also evidence of teamwork and communication skills here, and the applicant has also taken care to point that they are well-informed about the realities of a research career.

Materials Science and Engineering - As for a practical approach, a material scientist and engineer must be able to demonstrate a level of dexterity. My experimental skills are tested during my weekly lab sessions at school. The experiments carried out ranges from accurate titration to tedious production of Tollens' reagent. These sessions introduced me to the meticulous nature of experimentation and will be beneficial for my career. In addition, I joined a Carbon Dioxide Car Competition whereby students were assigned to create a carbon-dioxide-powered car that would propel maximally. Together with my teammates, we conducted research on accelerants that would enable the vessel to move farthest. By applying the principles of momentum, we added water into the vessel, so that it would travel longer. Despite not winning anything, my efforts did not go to waste as I was able to demonstrate my communicative skills by leading the experiment presentation for my team.

What makes this paragraph interesting?
Based on this paragraph, the applicant has demonstrated an awareness of the qualities required to be a successful material scientist (e.g. having fine motor skills), and provided some evidence proving he/she possess those abilities in their Chemistry practical sessions at school.

Other than that, the applicant showed that he/she can apply on their theoretical knowledge to tackle a challenge whilst displaying strong teamwork. These are traits highly valued in a science career.

Nevertheless, one way to further improve their writing would be for them to elaborate more about their competition experience. Perhaps they could talk more about why they think using water is the most viable solution to their problem, what would they have done differently if given a second chance, or even what other challenges they faced during the competition (such as tight deadlines or having a limited choice of materials).

Mathematics and Computer Science – The comple-
mentary impact between mathematics and computer
science is another reason I have chosen a joint degree.
Computer science relies on key concepts in mathem-
atics. This was clear when reading Algorithms by
Papadimitriou et al. and learning from Project Euler
about the shortest path problem, where brute force
can be avoided by updating the minimal weights.
Likewise, computing aids mathematical analysis
when systems are large and complex. For example, in
Palmer's lecture on The Butterfly Effect, a dynamic
computing programme was presented to visually
demonstrate a mathematically deduced tsunami.
And by participating in a scientific-based expedition
in the Forest of Mexico, I gained insight into the com-
plexities behind handling big data using statistics.

What makes this paragraph interesting?

Here the applicant takes care to acknowledge that scientific research requires the collaboration of experts from
interdisciplinary academic disciplines by effectively linking the different subjects of interest with each other.

Besides that, the applicant was able to justify the opinions
they have about their subject with an appropriate evidence from outside reading.

Extracurricular activities

Whilst reflections on your super-curricular activities
validate your claims on being a student that is keen to explore the breadth and depth of the subject, you need to
provide some evidence for your compatibility with the

teaching methods of your selected universities.

Do be cautious though, as mentioning extra-curricular activities are only useful if they align with the transferable skills that universities look out for, or if you explicitly explain how these experiences help to cultivate your interests towards your subject area.

Starting with soft skills, the common one which universities value include (but not limited to): communication, motivation, analytical skills, independence, leadership, collaboration/teamwork, resilience, problem-solving, self-discipline, time management/ability to meet deadlines, and critical thinking.

Taking that into account, a decent strategy going forward would be for you to place a greater emphasis on your mental growth as a result of your extra-curricular activities, rather than the nitty-gritty details of each event.

If you have been consistently engaged with your school or local community through volunteering or being a committee member of a club, you might have been challenged with demanding work timelines, had your leadership capabilities placed to a test, or you came to realise the power of compassion during your tenure.

Start-up founders and young inventors out there, this is the moment for you to shine and share more about how thinking inventively brought you to remarkable places and to achieve greater heights. If you coincidentally happen to be a part-time Starbucks barista hoping to read psychology, maybe you could link this with how it raised your curiosity in social anthropology and statistics.

You know yourself best, all you need to do is to reflect.

Examples
Here are a few examples of well-written and reflective statements.

My active personality meant that I always look for ways to extend my learning beyond the classroom. I have been a regular volunteer since the age of 13, which I was recognised for in both the local Newspaper and New Zealand National Broadcaster Seven Sharp, TVNZ. Being able to volunteer at many regional and national sporting events, and cultural festivals have put my communication skills into practice, and it has also helped me become more accepting of other cultures.

What makes this paragraph interesting?
In essence, the applicant's active participation in volunteering activities displayed wider spare time interests and provided evidence that he/she is an effective speaker as well as a keen learner.

Badminton has played a major role in my life for it has aided my fitness, shaped my critical and analytical mind, and gave me the confidence to face challenges. Being a captain in the badminton school team has strengthened my leadership, interpersonal skills as well as time management skills. I believe that these are the important traits of engineers that are highly sought after in the 21st century.

What makes this paragraph interesting?

As we previously discussed, the applicant has done well in explicating mentioning how his/her interest in playing badminton has allow them to develop the soft skills that are of high demand in an engineering career.

> *Aside from Mathematics, I am also very passionate in singing, and I was a bass vocalist in the Choir Club. Being the Vice President of Choir Club taught me how to communicate ideas effectively, be an active listener and be more accommodating while managing different team members.*

What makes this paragraph interesting?
It is essential to remember that your non-academic interests do not need to be something super impressive, as its sole purpose is to show that you have a life outside studying.

In this example, the reference made to their active engagement with the Choir Club is enough to reinforce the impression that the applicant is an avid team-player. It also obliquely suggests that the applicant possesses strong organisational and time management skills to juggle the heavy workload of their extracurricular activities along with their academic pursuits.

> *I've always found that the true test of my understanding of content was when I was able to explain it simply to others. I was eager to take this test a step further by joining 'Famelab', a science communication challenge. With a mind ready to learn, I revelled in the challenge of trying to explain scientific*

concepts to laymen without oversimplifying them. The process of choosing only what was necessary to include in my presentation enlightened me on the specific role different explanations played in contributing to the proper understanding of a concept. Emerging as a national finalist was only the icing of the chunky cake that embodied the invaluable communication skills I had acquired.

What makes this paragraph interesting?

The applicant's unique journey of participating in national public speaking competition suggests that he/she is not afraid to try something new, ultimately a person who is willing to step out of their comfort zone. The applicant also shows that they are able to work under stress as an effective communicator.

Poetry plays a crucial role in my life. Due to positive appraisal of my work, I was sponsored by college to participate in the Bridport Prize and the London Magazine Poetry Competition. It has allowed me to approach science from different philosophical standpoints, helping me perceive unusual links and generate interesting hypotheses on physics ideas.

What makes this paragraph interesting?

Impressively, the applicant has managed to link two interests in an unlikely manner and described how both of his/her passion complement each other to help them become a better physicist and a more profound thinker.

Sometimes, you got to take the lead

In certain occasions where your school lacks the resources, initiative or connections to offer such experiences, try to take that as a special challenge for yourself. This is a fairly unique learning opportunity for you.

Got a few friends interested in different facets of sciences? Cool. Get everyone together to start a new STEM club. All interested in machine learning instead? Register a robotics club then.

Are you a person who loves to teach, or you just enjoy sharing interesting things that you learnt about? Create a new podcast series, become a volunteer tutor at a local refugee shelter, or start a YouTube channel discussing your areas of interest.

Noticed your peers at school are also struggling to secure internships just like you? Take the initiative to propose a work observation placement scheme at your school.

All in all, be the person who takes the first step. It's the perfect time to get creative.

Gap years
If you are planning to take a whole year out before enrolling for university, it would be worth mentioning the plans you have in mind, and again, how do they relate to your course.

Proof that you have a life
While it is amazing for you to have numerous achievements and learnings in your academic pursuits, it is also ideal for admission tutors to know that you're capable of handling stress, especially due to the sheer workload presented by the STEM courses at top Russell Group universities. It essentially shows that you have a life outside

studying to relax and unwind, implying your ability to manage time effectively, another important skill that universities seek for.

Your extracurricular activities don't have to be anything super impressive. Do you play the piano? Or perhaps badminton? Maybe you knit, or go water-skiing every Sunday? Nice. No harm in briefly mentioning it, though it would be splendid if you could somehow link them to your subject.

This should only form approximately 5% (or less) of your total word count in your personal statement as most UK universities based their decisions completely on a student's academic merits.

Keeping a journal

As you probably would have realised, writing your personal statement involves digging a lot into your past and trying to draw relevant links to your subject area.

Hence, a tip to make your planning easier would be to keep a diary of your daily activities. Not only will this help you hone your writing skills and vocabulary size, but also guide you in your reflection on your experiences. This ultimately provides a chance to brainstorm new learning points about your subject, alongside your thoughts, feelings or questions throughout the process.

Not to mention, it's a safe platform for you to celebrate any of your successes.

Key takeaway messages

There are a few things to keep in mind if you want to write an excellent personal statement.

(1) Demonstrate a clear understanding about life as a scientist and the necessary traits to succeed in this career

(2) Most Russell Group universities prefer an academically-oriented personal statement

(3) Make sure each sentence exhibits your passion for the subject

(4) Try to link the contents of your personal statement as much as you can

(5) The greatest asset that you have is your mindset. This means YOU can make yourself stand out in so many ways by just thinking innovatively and positively

CHAPTER 4: SEALING THE DEAL

Now for the finale, there is no need for you to recap every single bit of your personal statement's content. This is simply because it does not add substantially to your profile.

Therefore, what else could you write about instead?

Study and/or professional career goals
Take around 10% of your character count to outline some of your perspective on how the general or scientific world works, linking them to your learning goals from this subject and course. And critically, how would this course help you create a positive impact for yourself and for your community (or in other words, why this course is important for you).

Maybe you don't have a defined job title in your mind at the moment, and that's okay. You could also write about the various possibilities that your subject opens yourself up to.

A Reader in Mathematics may aspire to solve one of the Millennium Prize Problems introduced by the Clay Mathematics Institute. A marine biologist could be passionate about maintaining ocean biodiversity and educating the general public about it. The list goes on.

Why you?

Technically speaking, the university is providing you with a service – it's called an education.

In return, an intriguing question you could keep in mind would be: what you could offer to your course and your university? Are you full of inventive ideas? Hoping to improve the student outreach at university? Or perhaps something relatively elementary such as planning to engage fully in what your course has to offer (including *cough* paying attention in lectures *cough*)?

As straightforward as you can be, summarise all the fundamentally positive qualities that you have, and indicate how it makes you a perfect fit for your course and soon-to-be learning community.

Biomedical Science - I am reasonably sure about my life mission. I found my calling when I interned at a hospital run by a community rehabilitation centre, named Anandwan, inhabiting roughly 5000 leprosy patients and differently enabled persons from economically challenged sections of the society. Witnessing the misery motivated me to choose medicine, but passion for science and fascination for research work instilled confidence that a course in Biomedical Sciences will be a better foundation to further my cause against the dire challenges facing human health. My career goal is to join academia and dedicate my life to biomedical research and teaching. My further ambition is to associate myself with the World Health Organisation (WHO) and contribute in health policy formulation to enable health benefits to reach the poorest and the farthest parts of the world.

What makes this paragraph interesting?
In this concluding paragraph, the applicant stressed that their fact-finding internship experience has reaffirmed their passion and motivation to pursue a career in their chosen subject. It suggests that the applicant has worked hard to inform themselves about the pathway forward as well as the new opinions that they have established about the significance of their subject.

> **Computer Science -** *My fascination with Computer Science has been developing ever since I took my first programming class in high school. Completing a bachelor's degree in Computer Science at a top UK university is the natural step in my career, given my interest in this discipline, and complementary mathematical and programming abilities. I am very determined to succeed in this degree course and I look forward to accomplishing my future professional goals, whether these entails working as a software developer, or doing research in the Computer Science field.*

What makes this paragraph interesting?
Just like how the applicant did, you can summarise how you have the passion and necessary core skills to succeed in your chosen university course.

It is perfectly fine if you are still uncertain about what you want to do after university, as part of your university journey is to help you answer that question. If that is the case, you can write about what doors your degree could open you up to.

Mechatronic Engineering - Being able to study in a top UK university will allow me to gain a broader perspective, as I look forward to meeting and learning along with a diverse community of people originating from different backgrounds and experiences. I believe this exposure will transform me into a highly adaptable and creative person who can develop products and services that offer a greater convenience to our society.

What makes this paragraph interesting?

Here the applicant provides a solid justification of why he/she wishes to study specifically at a top UK university, helping the reader to understand how this aligns with the applicant's ambitions and/or career goals.

One way to further improve this statement would be for the applicant to describe how the university's degree course, in particular, aligns with the future interests. But don't forget that different UK universities may have a different course structure despite sharing the same degree title. Hence, conducting a thorough research will be mandatory.

Key takeaway messages

Your final paragraph may summarise:

(1) How your chosen degree will help you achieve your career goals

(2) All the positive attributes that make you a suitable candidate for this course

(3) How the style of education at your chosen universities can help you develop your intellectual curiosity

CHAPTER 5: CASE IN POINT

Congratulations, you have made it this far.

Now that you have read about the various tips and tricks that you could employ to help your personal statement stand out, here are a few full-length samples of successful personal statements to help you consolidate your learnings.

Based on what we have discussed in the previous chapters, have a think about how each paragraph and sentence have *added value* to you, as a reader, to better understand the applicant and their motivations for studying their subject.

The general take-home message for each example is that – strong personal statements typically exhibit how an applicant's views and mastery of their subject evolved over time. The style of writing often provides hints of the subject-oriented themes and patterns that the applicant gained an awareness of and began to investigate. These are then effectively connected to their super-curricular activities, with a detailed account on how these experiences reinforced their passion and allowed their ideas to develop.

In short, it is a short story about their journey in academic development that was first ignited through curiosity, ultimately culminating into their application to study that subject at university-level.

Life Sciences (Biochemistry)

Richard Dawkins debates the idea of altruism within species in The Selfish Gene: whether our selfish or selfless behaviour is down to nature or nurture then stating that in essence, our genes are responsible for the behaviour that enables an individual or a species to survive. The thought that such minute entities determine almost anything from phenotype to behaviour enthrals me.

In my studies of Biology A level, I was introduced to the concepts of transcription and translation and discovered how one single error could change the entire life of a person. Realising how unfair it is that the course of a person's life is decided before they are born prompted me to deepen my understanding of the involvement of these processes in various diseases. To further understand how they aid in other processes such as viral replication, I attended a lecture at St. Mary's Hospital about "Predicting and Preventing Infectious Diseases," which focused mainly on HIV and how we are able to control the disease using Antiretroviral Therapy (ART) and highlighted its dangers and limitations. What I found particularly interesting was that the only man that has been cured, received transplanted bone marrow which fortunately had the delta-32 mutation on the CCR5 receptor protein, preventing other viruses from entering the host cell due to the different shape of the protein receptor. This made me wonder whether it is possible to simulate a similar effect with synthetic drugs that would act in a similar way.

The future of scientific research in areas such as infectious diseases is promising. The RV144 trial statistics about the action of HIV vaccines led me to question why some treatments, such as vaccines, work and some don't. I realised the importance of chemical principles when designing effective drugs, with the omission of testing for optical activity leading to a worldwide Thalidomide catastrophe. I was fascinated to see that the teratogenic form of Thalidomide was able to evade the efflux transport system thus remaining within the cell and causing oxidative stress that led to limb deformities. Through one particular New Scientist, "everything you need to know about 3-parent babies," I discovered that the aim of this technique was to avoid the inheritance of the genetic disorder called Leigh Syndrome which was passed down from the mitochondrial DNA of the mother. I conducted further research to learn that Leigh Syndrome could also be inherited as an autosomal recessive neurometabolic disorder which is sex-linked. I am fascinated by the level of research that goes into new treatments to ensure their success which is yet another reason to study Biochemistry.

The completion of the Human Genome Project allows exciting new advances in personalised medicine as well as genetic engineering. Bryan Appleyard's remarks in a podcast challenged my opinions on the use of genetics as he highlighted that consumerism of the knowledge of genetics brings about a totalitarian perception by the public. The podcast revealed that understanding the biochemistry of phenylketonuria (PKU) allows treatments to be developed. The pivotal role of biochemistry fuels my desire to play a part in future research as visible positive results are obtained that have direct impact on health and society.

Outside of academic life, studying the flute has honed my ability to multitask and pay attention to detail, which are put to practice during my weekly orchestral practice. Being a member of the Air Cadet Organisation, I had the opportunity to gain many valuable skills such as teamwork and communication which enabled me to apply to be part of the Head Girl team at school. Studying languages allows me to immerse myself in different cultures as well as challenging my thought process, teaching me to approach problems in various ways.

I believe that my self-driven motivation and competence makes me a suitable candidate for this course, and I am prepared to face any challenges with a positive attitude.

Physical Sciences (Physics)

The emission and absorption lines on the echelle spectrum which recorded the periastron passage of the highly eccentric Classical Be binary star Delta Scorpii may look like the scribbles of a child, but to me, they hold a world of wonder. It elucidates how the tidal force due to gravity induces the accretion of matter around the star which results in the formation of the circumstellar envelope. I researched this phenomenon during my internship at the University of Malaya. During this internship I was able to appreciate the centrality of Physics in explaining natural phenomena both theoretically and mathematically.

Studying the articles written on L'observataire de Paris helped me understand how the axial rotation of a star increases in a low metallicity environment. This made me infer that all B stars with fast axial rotations at birth would undergo the Be phenomenon. However, upon further research, I discovered evidence of fast rotating stars that lack a decreation disk. This shows that although axial rotation plays a fundamental role in the genesis of Be stars, it is not the sole physical process involved.

The fact that most Be stars appear in multiple star systems

made me think that the exchange of mass between stars could cause the formation of a protoplanetary disk. Reading papers published by Cornell University regarding Delta Scorpii during the periastron passage and comparing the radial velocity and visual continuum with other stellar spectrums taken over the past 10.5 years showed me the clear changes in disk radius of the star. Reading "Stellar Evolution at Low Metallicity under the influence of binary interaction and rotation" by S.E de Main taught me to mathematically predict the exchange of kinetic energy, mass and angular momentum between stars in a closed binary. This made me conclude that the interaction of stars in a binary system may be one of the causes for the anisotropic gaseous envelope surrounding Be stars.

The research I conducted helped me enhance my mathematical and programming skills as I used software such as IRAF to model and measure the radial velocity, visual continuum, and line flux of hydrogen alpha, beta and gamma as well as Helium-6678 and Helium-4388 of Delta Scorpii during the periastron passage. There was a slight deviation between the radial velocity curve of hydrogen alpha and helium, indicating that the orbit is unstable. This could be the result of a third companion star being ejected from its orbit, proving that Delta Scorpii may have previously been a triple star system. Interning with a professor made me realize that physics requires intensive analysis and evaluation of data to find patterns in complex problems. Attending national level chess competitions taught me to analyse difficult positions and evaluate the best solution possible.

While volunteering to teach the victims affected by the East Coast floods that struck Malaysia in November 2015, my eyes were opened to the catastrophic effects of climate change. I undertook an Extended Project Qualification to investigate the causes of the increase in monsoon rainfall intensities. Initial research led me to believe that they were the result of global temperature increase, which caused a dramatic shift in El Nino Southern Oscillation as shown by a study done by NOAA-NCDC which compared global precipitation against temperature anomalies. However, monsoon anomalies could also be naturally caused by the Himalayan uplift. The increased precipitation could result in a positive feedback loop as it causes erosion of the mountain which affects tectonic evolution by focusing and increasing exhumation.

The different perspectives on this phenomenon showed me the importance of challenging theories and basing conclusions on accurate experimental results. This encouraged me to question the reliability of everything I read and I hope by pursuing a degree in physics, I am able to provide answers to very important and impactful questions.

Engineering (Chemical Engineering)
Standing in front of conveyor belts and machinery, I scrutinised the stages in which raw ingredients were being processed into various products after clearing stringent quality control. I thought about ways to improve these processes, especially in the regulation of operating conditions to enhance the rate of reaction and yield of products. I see these as part of my future work responsibilities.

My interest in chemical engineering was stimulated after witnessing how an indigenous community in Sarawak suffered from a high mortality rate from water-borne diseases due to the lack of access to clean drinking water. Amongst the things I am determined to do is to invent affordable water purifiers to meet people's needs. An extract from "Reader's Digest" regarding applications of silver nanoparticles with antimicrobial properties in water purification, together with hours of online research, strengthened my interest in combining silver nanoparticles and nanocellulose from palm oil fibre to purify water. Silver nanoparticles, which can be synthesised through the reduction of silver ions by natural leaves' extracts, are impregnated onto cellulose fibre at room temperature. Thus, the people in developing nations will be empowered to produce clean water independently. To me, a chemical engineer must constantly strive to raise living standards through innovation.

Discussing cooking in terms of numbers and chemistry may sound bizarre, but cooking does involve a series of chemical reactions and measurements. Being inspired by this correlation, I worked in a snack kiosk and a palm oil mill. I was amazed by the parallel between the mechanism in popping popcorn and the extraction of oil from tough palm oil husks, especially in processes such as pressing and steam injection. Precise regulation of temperature, pressure and moisture content is a prerequisite in breaking the hard shell of popcorn and oil husks perfectly. An intriguing aspect of the palm oil mill operation is its self-sustainability. The fibre left after the pressing process is used as the starter fuel of the boiler and thus reduces the reliance on non-renewable fossil fuels. Insight gained on the use of fibre in industry prompted me to research further on its other applications. I was satisfied after discovering that fibre could act as an adsorbent in removing heavy metal ions. I realised the significant role of a chemical engineer in transforming waste into useful assets to conserve dwindling resources. I also had hands-on practice in conducting quality control tests on fresh fatty acid content in palm oil. This tedious experience impressed on me the importance of automated machines in taking the drudgery out of the industry.

Aside from academic pursuits, I enjoy outdoor activities. Taking up the role of President of the Scout Society was challenging, especially during the annual Campfire when I was the logistics manager leading a committee of forty and was in charge of every member's safety. This experience developed my interpersonal skills as I learnt to accept criticism positively and negotiate with others in decision-making. Being Vice President of the Engineering Society, I actively joined various competitions such as the water boat competition, where I learnt to twist the propeller blade to its optimum blade angle, and the innovation project where I created springy shoes. My involvement in different activities gave me exposure to the different fields of engineering. My intense desire to learn Mathematics and Science was rewarded when I received High Distinctions in the National Chemistry Quiz and in ICAS Science held by the University of New South Wales.

Studying in the UK, where I can exchange ideas of technical expertise and be exposed to cutting-edge research and equipment will be an invaluable experience. I anticipate using this degree course to explore the various aspects of this wide-ranging field before deciding on a specific career in chemical engineering.

Technology and Mathematics (Computer Science)
My interest in the field of computer science and artificial intelligence (AI) was sparked when I first came across a news article on Deepmind's AlphaGo programme defeating the Go world champion Lee Sedol in early 2016. I was

fascinated by the fact that a computer was able to outplay a human expert in such a complex game using learning algorithms rather than brute force computing. It is exciting to imagine that a general learning algorithm could be created, and that it would help us to push the boundaries of our knowledge.

My first engagement with computer science was in college. I was involved in a project about creating a programme that takes student attendances using barcode scanners to scan their student IDs. Through this experience, I was introduced to the basics of programming. To build upon my knowledge, I have also read A.B Downey's "How to Think like a Computer Scientist". I enjoyed going through the problem sets in the book and challenging myself to come up with solutions to each of them. Besides that, a project that I enjoyed working on was an AI programme that plays tic-tac-toe. This experience has taught me to be meticulous when designing algorithms, as I had to consider all the possible situations that the AI could be in, and how best to respond to each of them. I also learnt about the importance of using simulations in predicting the effectiveness of each possible move the AI could play. This project gave me a glimpse of how brute-force methods are used in developing AI.

Recently I read the book "Complexity: A Guided Tour" by Melanie Mitchell, and I enjoyed it. In the book, one thing I found interesting is that biologists are borrowing the ideas of computation & information processing to explain the complex behaviour seen in natural systems like ant colonies. Moreover, I was fascinated by how computer scientists, being inspired by evolution & natural selection, came out with the idea of genetic algorithms, which are capable of mating and evolving computer programmes. This approach produces unique solutions that we humans may never think about. Through this book, I saw how the fields of computer science and biology influence each other. This versatile nature of computer science is particularly appealing to me, as it can be applied to other academic fields to solve problems.

I believe that, through my A-levels studies, I have developed an analytical mind to solve problems. Through mathematics, I have learnt to break problems down into multiple parts and to take a step-by-step approach in solving it. Meanwhile in Physics, I have learnt about the importance of creating mathematical models to explain physical phenomena. Also, being someone who likes mathematics, I undertook an independent study in Further Mathematics after my A2's, and I have thoroughly enjoyed reading the statistics modules. Among them, I find linear regression the most interesting because it allows us to make predictions based on existing data. I believe that studying these subjects will help me lay a good foundation for studying computer science.

I was the vice president of the engineering club in college, and together with my team I have led several club-wide projects, which include building mini catapults and simple electronic sensors. Moreover, serving as a cell group leader in my church's youth ministry has helped me develop my communication and leadership skills. Representing my school in football has also taught me the importance of teamwork. These qualities will be useful in group projects.

I would love to study in the UK for it has so many beautiful landscapes, great cities, and medieval towns to visit.

In the future, I aspire to be an active researcher in the field of AI and hopefully one day be able to participate in creating general-purpose AI. For that reason, I look forward to studying computer science at a university level.

Yinx 2020

CHAPTER 6: FINAL WORDS OF WISDOM

Welcome to the final chapter of this book. Now that you (hopefully) have a better understanding of the personal statement writing technique, with your mind flowing with loads of ideas and you're all hyped up to begin...

That's lovely! But before you set out to draft your first essay, I have a few final tips that I believe are worth keeping in mind:

Know your ~~enemy~~ audience

If you know neither yourself nor your enemy,
you will always endanger yourself.

If you only know yourself, but not your enemy,
you may win or may lose.

If you know your enemies and know yourself,
you can win a hundred battles without a single loss.

Sun Tzu, 600 BC
Chinese general and military strategist

It always pays to be self-aware, knowing your strengths and improvement points.

But that's not enough.

The person you are trying to impress is the admission tutor(s) themselves, and to a certain extent – if you want "to know your ~~enemy~~ audience, you must ~~become your enemy~~ think from their perspective."

How?

Easy. First things first, you need to be certain of the subject area that you're applying for, and your target universities very well.

A good way to get to know more about your top course choices would be to attend university open days. If you are an international student, you can always clarify on the entry requirements or what the admissions tutors generally look for by emailing or calling the university's admissions department. Some universities may also explicitly list down the characteristics of an ideal applicant on their website, if that may provide some guidance with your application.

Alternatively, connecting to current students or alumni via social networks such as LinkedIn are also viable action plans.

Presentation
Just like a regular essay you had to write for schoolwork, it is imperative for you to consider how your materials are presented to your reader.

With that in mind, best practice involves outlining a concrete plan for your personal statement. A well-structured essay essentially translates into you being able to meticulously address your reader's logic, giving you full control of what the admissions tutors need to know about you, and in what order they received each detail.

So before jumping into a 4K-character writing spree, start with this: determine the various topics or experiences that you intend to write about. Using that outline, divide them into separate paragraphs to ensure an organized flow of information.

In general, the outline should consist of:

1. The opening paragraph explaining your initial motivations to study your chosen subject.

2. Three to four paragraphs demonstrating your academic interests by writing about your super-curricular activities and how they helped to further develop your knowledge and excitement for your subject.

3. A concise closing statement summarising your extra-curricular initiatives and how your chosen subject aligns with your future career/life goals.

Other fairly obvious things to keep an eye out for: spelling, grammar, punctuation, and making sure that all abbreviations and acronyms are clearly defined. You know the drill.

Once you have completed your first draft, read each paragraph aloud. The aim of this is to ensure a coherent set of ideas from start to end. And from there, edit and repeat until you're satisfied.

Writing style and tone

Alongside keeping your writing style consistent with the academic English format, this is no time for you to downplay yourself.

This essentially means that you ought to make use of *simple* vocabulary that conveys a *positive* tone, ultimately selling the best version of yourself.

One way to achieve this would be for you to try beginning each paragraph of your personal statement with the most outstanding or extraordinary piece of information you possess, coupled with an appropriate set of evidence(s).

But don't forget to respect the fine line between arrogance and modesty. Do maintain a humble tone and show a reflective mindset in your writing. Admissions tutors (and basically no one in general) likes a person who brags.

Seeking feedback
This is probably the trickiest bit.

Although it may seem like a good idea to speak to as many people as you can to gather different opinions on how to improve the quality of your work, it would be paradoxically counterproductive for you to try to incorporate advice from 55 different people, for example.

The general rule of thumb would be to prioritise which feedback you attend to, depending on the individual who provided it.

Feedback from schoolteachers *with* previous experience in mentoring students for university applications, current students, or alumni who successfully gained a place at your first-choice university would make the most sensible people for you to seek advice from.

One more criterion though, get the *ruthless* one. You will need someone who is unafraid to drill into and stress test all your written statements. You're way better off getting yourself roasted sooner than later.

On the other hand, if your family and friends do not fall under any of those categories, a good topic for a productive discussion would be to pinpoint the various personal attributes or soft skills that showcases your suitability to the university's course instead.

Treasuring individuality and diversity
It is clear that the admissions office can receive both an excellent personal statement as well as a poorly written one every year.

Nevertheless, it is important for you to recognise that a perfect personal statement simply *does not* exist, not even an ideal applicant!

As highlighted by the University of Oxford, universities seek to establish a diverse community of bright and unique individuals. Taking that into consideration, admissions tutors do not have a checklist of mandatory achievements and milestones, or specific keywords and phrases to select the right applicant to interview/extend an offer to.

No, you do not need to be a founder of your own business since the age of sixteen. Not all successful applicants were gold medallists for the International Physics Olympiad (let alone a participant), and you certainly do not need to be the Grand Prize winner at the annual Google Science Fair (although being able to achieve one, or if not all, of these would be a legendary feat that is definitely worth mentioning).

The key is for you to match your materials with the selection criteria published by your university, which are showcasing academic potential and enthusiasm for your course.

That being said, this should also give you a very good reason to not lie or exaggerate your stories. I know that you are a creative person, but this presents little to no advantage towards yourself and to the admission tutors. A brilliant scientist could lose his or her career within an instance if they were caught falsifying their data or plagiarising a peer's work. I don't want you to go down that route, and practising good habits begins right now!

So, God forbid writing about a book you have not read or analysed in great detail, together with not having formulated a few interesting discussion points – especially if interviews form part of the candidate selection process, they can catch you out pretty easily.

An additional good tip would be to try avoiding reading someone else's personal statement until you've written your first draft, thereby helping to keep your writing style as original as possible.

Starting early
Here's a solid fact – just like your career, it is never too early to start thinking about your personal statement, even if you're still in your final year of GCSEs, on a gap year, or just beginning your pre-university syllabus.

Although, you don't have to start the official writing yet.

Instead, spend the time to explore around the different STEM subjects, find out more about what you and everyone else still don't know about, ask yourself more questions, and be curious!

This is an invaluable opportunity to cultivate your academic interests, and to build up your profile. One way to create an action plan would be to ask yourself: what are your future goals, what is your ideal (or dream, if you dare) job, what problem(s) do you aspire to address or solve, which subjects do you enjoy the most at school, how do they relate to your degree, and what are the knowledge and skill sets necessary to meet your personal and professional targets?

Once the summer before the university applications season arrives, take all the time you need to craft your masterpiece.

A realistic and (probably) accurate fact – your initial drafts are not going to be great, so just get started anyway! Most writers don't get things right in their first round, but majority of them are excellent "re-writers".

With that being said, there is no need for you to stress yourself out too much about this. Start with a plan and a great determination, and soon enough you'll be submitting your final version with the wonderful feeling of satisfaction.

All the best there, you got this.

IF PERSONAL STATEMENTS WERE HONEST #6

REFERENCES

1. University of Cambridge. (2019) *Application statistics*

2. Imperial College London. (2019) *Department of Chemical Engineering*

3. Von Stumm, S., Hell, B. & Chamorro-Premuzic, T. (2011) The hungry mind: Intellectual curiosity is the third pillar of academic performance. *Perspectives on Psychological Science.* 6(6), 574-588.

4. Harvard Business Review. (2018) *Why curiosity matters*

ACKNOWLEDGEMENTS

This book would not have become a reality without the inspiration and contributions from so many people. Where do I even start?

First of all, I would like to thank my parents, for their constant encouragement for me to pursue something I deeply care about.

Next, I would like to thank my friends, Jedidiah Cheung and Chris Kwok, for instilling the idea that writing a short book is extremely possible, and all it takes for one to accomplish that would be to brainstorm a topic and get started. Totally worth that coffee chat at Pret guys!

Not to mention, I must thank everyone who have kindly contributed their personal statements for this book. A big *gracias* to (in no particular order) Anamaria Grijincu, Lim En May, Soumya Sharma, Do Wenrei, Lee Ee Hooi, Ng Chuan Jeen, Ngu Ming Jiun, Bianca Teodora Catea, Ng Eu Keat, Jieni Wang, Vanessa Tang, Kitty Lei, Yanda Wong, Lee Jian Hao, Low Jess Lyn, Shantralmalar Rasa, Low Kian Chong, Diyanah Kamarul Azman, Sufia Faisal, Jesidhn Pillai, Jane Lai, Edna Au, and Bryan Beh. This book would not have existed without your help!

Moving on, there is simply no denial that I must thank the one and only Tan Ying Xin, for her wonderful comic illustrations and creativity. You inject so much passion into whatever you do, and I could not have asked for anything better than what you have created for this book. Keep drawing, dear friend!

And finally, I have to thank my close friend, Isabelle Tan, for her support in making this book a reality. You have done so much for me as a friend, and I really don't know how much to thank you for that, honestly.

ABOUT THE AUTHOR

Bianca Khor holds a Bachelor of Science (Honours) in Biochemistry from Imperial College London. Prior to entering university, she grew up in Kuala Lumpur, Malaysia and completed her A Levels in Kolej Tuanku Ja'afar, where she was awarded the Overall Academic Excellence Book Prize within her cohort. She is now a writer and is passionate about travelling, stories, and finding ways to give back to the community.

Printed in Great Britain
by Amazon